United States Capitol

Julie Murray

Abdo
US LANDMARKS
Kids

abdopublishing.com

Published by Abdo Kids, a division of ABDO, PO Box 398166, Minneapolis, Minnesota 55439.
Copyright © 2017 by Abdo Consulting Group, Inc. International copyrights reserved in all countries.
No part of this book may be reproduced in any form without written permission from the publisher.

Printed in the United States of America, North Mankato, Minnesota.

102016
012017

THIS BOOK CONTAINS
RECYCLED MATERIALS

Photo Credits: Alamy, AP Images, iStock, Library of Congress, Shutterstock, U.S. Capitol,
©Chris Parypa Photography p.21 / Shutterstock.com

Production Contributors: Teddy Borth, Jennie Forsberg, Grace Hansen

Design Contributors: Christina Doffing, Candice Keimig, Dorothy Toth

Publisher's Cataloging in Publication Data

Names: Murray, Julie, author.

Title: United States Capitol / by Julie Murray.

Description: Minneapolis, Minnesota : Abdo Kids, 2017 | Series: US landmarks |
   Includes bibliographical references and index.

Identifiers: LCCN 2016943935 | ISBN 9781680809152 (lib. bdg.) |
   ISBN 9781680796254 (ebook) | ISBN 9781680796926 (Read-to-me ebook)

Subjects: LCSH: United States Capitol (Washington, D.C.)--Juvenile literature. |
   Washington (D.C.)--Buildings, structures, etc.--Juvenile literature.

Classification: DDC 975.3--dc23

LC record available at http://lccn.loc.gov/2016943935

Table of Contents

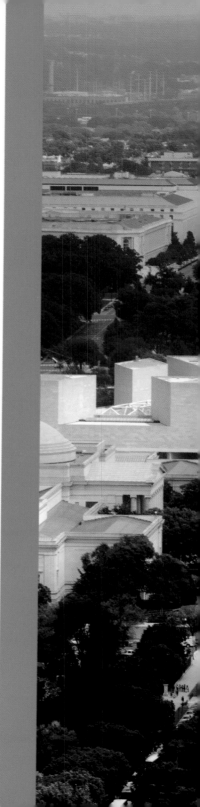

United States Capitol

The US Capitol is in

Washington D.C.

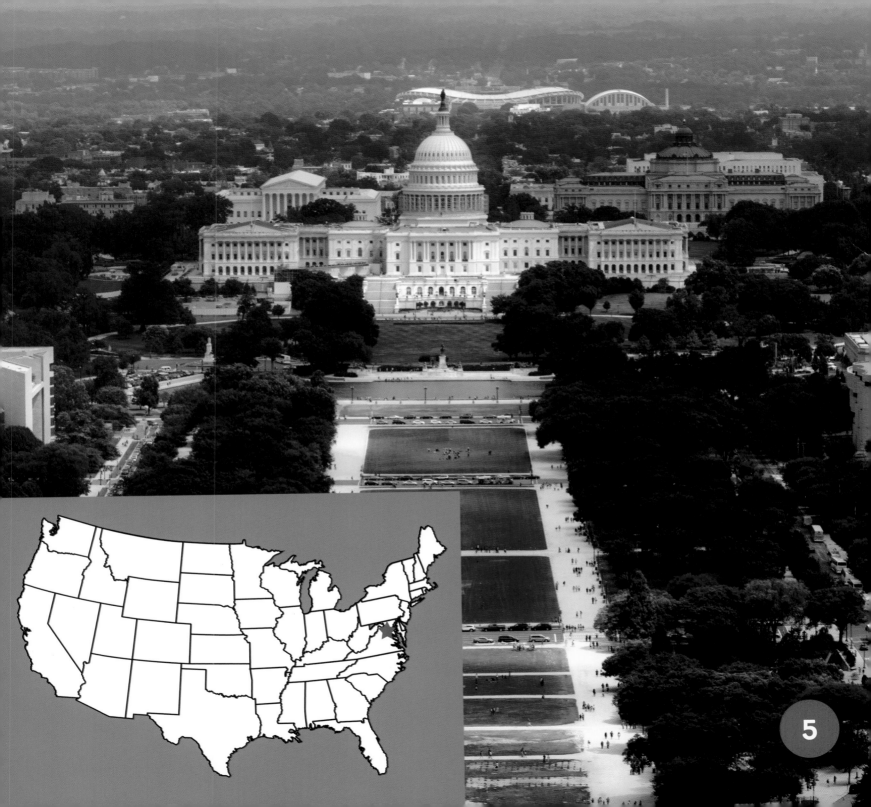

Congress works here.

They make laws.

Building it began in 1793.

It has changed over the years.

Many new areas were added.

Dec 23
1887

Today it has 540 rooms.

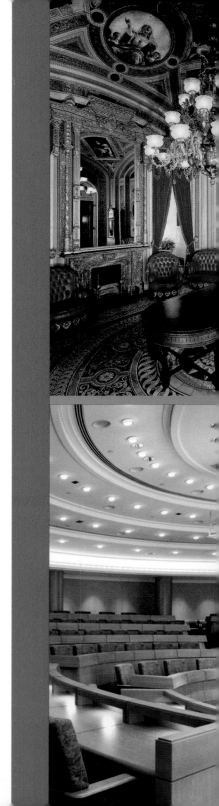

15

The Capitol is 288 feet
(88 m) tall.

A dome is on top. A statue sits on it. It stands for freedom.

Many people visit each year.

More Facts

George Washington laid the first cornerstone

the dome is almost 4,500 tons (4 million kg) of iron

burned in the War of 1812

658 windows (108 in dome)

Glossary

Congress
the group of people who make laws in the United States.

Washington D.C.

D.C.
short for District of Columbia.

Index

abdokids.com

Use this code to log on to abdokids.com and access crafts, games, videos, and more!

Abdo Kids Code:
UUK9152